Lives

By the same author:

Poems for Peckleton (1980)
The History of Market Bosworth (1983)
The Field of Redemore (1990)
A Study of Llewelyn Powys (1991)

Lives

PETER FOSS

HEADLAND

First published in 1995

by

HEADLAND PUBLICATIONS

North Wales and Wirral

Tŷ Coch, Galltegfa, Llanfwrog,
Ruthin, Clwyd. LL15 2AR

and

38 York Avenue, West Kirby,
Wirral, Merseyside L48 3JF

A CIP record for this book is available
from the British Library.

ISBN
0 903074 68 0

Some of these poems have previously appeared in magazines
including *Spectrum*, *Outcrop* and *Other Poetry*.

Typeset, designed and printed by
Nichols Print, Heswall. Wirral. L60 7RB

Contents

To

Peter and Kathy Miles

THE INTERSECTION

What I will most recall is the drug of cold;
faces the streets shed at the intersection,
and a kind of *leviathan* I couldn't coax.

On roofs and ruined churches was planked iron;
the realms of delicate railings wandered awry
to the far yards with their drab sheds and dye-works;

at every crossing where the iced asphalt jangled
whirred pumps and tankers, the gauges mounting
through fractions; engaged engines; contraptions.

After a while, whiteness and nothing spoken –
a reflection of boredom perhaps, and vacant fancies.
From a crowded carriage where the drained faces foundered

I looked out strangely at the neat cut of a park
uncertain above the siding's vegetation.
And at night when I still remember the tension

at a crossing where two lines meet, the long
lighted necklace sliding away to the horizon,
I stood in the mask of sulphur whispering 'Go'.

Lives

These too were young,
lived life in their jumpers and tweeds.
They stood, hands in pockets, in doorways,
or arms entwined,
walked together down Berlin streets.

With fine thoughts, his head full of music,
this man looked dreamily across the marshes
from his mill.
Another played father at a party
in Manhattan, but bolder, ambitious,
a poet with skin.

They are all dead now,
and I am left with pictures,
sitting by myself and finding them over again
in books.

All those days too were lived closely
in the minute's marrow
as mine are, these slight, slow hours now.

IRIS

I see in the yellow keel a vein of light
the blue boldens, the pale violet tongue
like a lick of fire where the coal eases
in a real fire, the flame a flower's fan.

This shows too in shoots of blue and gold;
three-petalled, hafted, stigmas like feathered scoops;
the three spear-leaves folded on the stalk,
the sun-tinged lepidoptera's wings.

I find in its blazon the cast of a quick heat;
below, a toiling, surer chemistry.
I give you the coronet of this cobalt flower
in threes in purple paper for your keep.

All Queens of Heaven held fire or a flower
in knots of three: strength, wisdom, wealth.
Mine may be simpler than the sacrament and dove;
blue is for faith and yellow is for love.

AUBADE

In the white dawn where the window's screen faced us,
crazed with the night's frost in late October,
we woke, in love, to the same spare concerto.

Along the passages these sounds of Mozart
like resolutions of all fear and folly
merged with the morning's drone and crying kettle.

From gantry doors where the bleak concrete stairwells
defined the contours of the fractured city,
there crept the children that the streets devour.

Here, opaque in the window's sudden glare,
beside the trays of cups, the night's sweet litter,
our love was nourished by the music's virtue.

You lay, your arms outstretched like Goya's *Maja,*
then rose to bathe, and I to smoke and dress.
Outside the city hummed its only solace

for the black poor, the lovers and the lonely;
whilst in the spaces where the ginnels meet the crescents
the palest dawn uncovers Mozart's children.

HOME FROM HOME*

Something like that,
for a moment looking apart at the sun's dazzle
on the pull of the current;
overhead the crazy shrieks of gulls
rattling in Netpool.

I took it all in like another kind of dream:
the bridge, a renovated mill,
the last light harrying the tide,
whitewash on crumbled stone and mortar like icing.
And here, in focus, neck against estuary,
your face unsaying, bewildered;
myself, indulging only the salt taste
of bladderwrack on the breeze.

The idea was enough: dolls' houses
nudging each other down to the curious Mwldan;
scarlet pimpernels, strawberry-dots crowding every crack
in the town wall; and all the unpainted
precarious clutter of that town on its cleft.
Something like that.

* *Cardigan 1981-2*

CHILD

I would want to make a copy of that face:
the lifted gold-leaf hair of that ruffled head;
hands morticed like a saint's
(harbouring his catapult);
the O-shaped gape of wonder
at gull and shard and sheerness.

I would want to catch the turn of two eyes
upward, like an ecstasy at the moment of craving
to leap – but collected for an ingenuous smile
instead; of a blue sleeveless coat
on miniature limbs; the child's play
of casual apt words spoken
for their own sake;
the delight of wind and sun
and the spacious scabious.

THE PICTURE

There must be a picture hidden away somewhere,
its gilt frame gone green, its edges frayed.
Across the piles of paste dark shadows
show the eyes, and the mouth is crazed.
Where the smooth cheeks should be the canvas cracks,
and through the warp and woof
the back-board's sutures spill a viscous sap.

It's still there no doubt, high in a loft
where everything's pushed that the years
use and leave, this picture
of the other he that's lost.

That's real though,
where the paint boils and burns;
and quietly downstairs
this thick blank skin's on show.

THE FALL

How innocent we were then. Before the fall
we wandered freely in the garden of fear.
We made a luxury of all that food
not thinking it was jealousy and gall.
We didn't look then at the bark's intermesh,
finding grimaces and grief in the knots and scars.
We thought ourselves into a trance of experience
and turned back freely all the awkward brambles.
All the years helped towards the blood's dream –
a secret fullness drawing to a head.
Everywhere there was fruit. One day the sweet
berries were soft to our taste,
disgorged among the garden's indifferent arbours.

MWNT

We climbed there too, held hands, kissed,
lay back on the still side, loved
the slow time that held us in its heat,
where the wind was not to reach us
and only the shake of the surf and the gulls'
shriek came to us there –
We were the ones once adventuring
those crag-paths on the other side
as the two up there you see,
and balanced on the hill's back's
razor-ridge, me daringly,
you fearfully,
above the trusted sea.

Even the little boy in his anorak
with abandoned wonder
looks inland to the cwm and limekiln,
averting to the angle of his eye
the incomprehensible cliff.
Somewhere or other, like the space
where the plover lifts upward on the wind,
was that strange newness;
while now in earshot from another place
the cark of bitterness stirs
words like knives
scarring a frightened face.

A PHOTOGRAPH: CHINGLE HALL, 1980

A frost's sharp light; myself, shy of the lens,
took up a pick and posed –
one of the monkish ghosts from the stone moat.
She clung (clings now), searching for my smile,
breathing the air I cloud, holding my coat.

The shutter that always lies, makes one
of two, takes pick for stick and gaberdine
for cloak, whitens my quizzing face,
parades the ties –
her arm in mine, her look, her loving lies.

Only the once, placed indivisibly.
Around us, all the exercise of love:
the days, the nights, the empty unknown streets
we wandered through,
because our hands were held,
our hearts were lost...

How wise it was, that look into the lens,
the wry effacement challenging the frost.

THE SUMMER OF THE NEW ELIZABETHANS

Out again come the flags and the commemoratives:
mugs 'not necessarily well-designed or of high quality';
spoons and tins and a Coronation crown
in cane by Charlie Crampton; and again
the bunting and the floats and real enthusiasm...

We didn't honestly think it would be like this.
Even the sun seems to condone it and smiles;
and after all, once it was something else again
before the *ennui* set in and that sixties guile.

The living was harder then and on the line –
less expected and more things saved and valued;
and even I remember the dull green and the races
and a table spread by the railings, bus-rides and prizes.

I didn't quite gather what it was about,
but what does that matter? The jewels were a feature
still to visit and gawp at; ceremony
bore the character of a dream into which we escaped–
in a way, not for us at all, but a spectacle
of what we actually meant if we only knew it.

And here it comes again in the nostalgic seventies
(an anachronism hardly believable really),
with our oil and inflation and top-level meetings,
European commissions, blow-outs and muggings and punk;

and our love of sifting it all through again,
re-tasting it, testing it, savouring the flavour
on our inquisitive palates, and yearning for yesterday
and things so unreal, so *passé*.

Yes, I can't help it either – I love these images.
And it's now more our own thing, more than it was;
we've made it personal, perhaps because of the telly;
we bother with streamers and like to delight the kiddies.
We are the ones who decide to make it mythic.

HINCKLEY DISPLAYED

Undecided as to what
In plainest terms it cannot be,
This town the visitor forgot
Relinquishes identity.

No love lost here, or any such
Compassion, sentiment or grace;
Not even years of toil can touch
A heart once hardened to this place.

Mere trade, unsubtle, understood,
Is all these buildings meant to show;
Obtusely confident that mud
Be made to give the gold its glow.

Dissenting chapels keep from view
Their loyalties in common faith;
Their knitting congregations knew
A stubborn privacy was safe.

In yards and jitties where the frames
To reddened hands would stitch up socks,
A never-ending clatter names
The kind of life that's lived by clocks.

No room for mystery or doubt,
or art or love or thoughtful things;
A pragmatism so devout
Neutralizes deeper stings.

And some are happy, most content,
with brick and grit and garden plots;
A small tradition that has lent
To non-description beauty-spots.

But beauty on occasion blooms
In modest, meagre, common ground;
And wonder even decks the looms,
And love in little often found.

A chapel old in wood and slate,
Fuses human faith in bricks;
Its gallery and pews dictate
What can in practice well be mixed:

A scale both human and divine,
As long as man is never lost;
He is the measure for his time
And he it is must count the cost.

Thus the benefactions stand
Endowed by none of real note;
They merely made their business grand,
And founded libraries for folk.

And so the silver band proclaims,
Processioning down Castle Street,
An affirmation none disdains
That small is best and brick is neat.

STOCKERSTON*

Nestling close as though grown there
On the wooded hill, this hall, this church;
Alike removed from human care
And long survived our will to search.

But search we do. A lane through fields
From corner and cottages leads us there;
Randomly the landscape yields
Sheep and pasture, earth and air.

As though opposed in competition
Brick and stone stand sentinel;
But in the wind a still condition
Speaks of love locked on that hill.

Brick hall, stone church, some countryside;
A place to live perhaps and die.
The marble slab discreetly hides
The bones that once went riding by.

One lady; knight and wife; some more;
As well perfected in brass or stone;
A harvesting of Nature's store
in life when they were more than bone.

But these are nothing. Because a place
Draws us along a lonely lane,
We are the ones now given grace
By their existences to gain.

Why is this, when the times are changed?
I mean, what gives us rights to be
Here, where others waxed and waned,
And we seek only harmony?

Exactly that; they justify
Myself and others, thought and act;
Their love is ours, and we supply
Feeling which makes them more than fact.

Hall, church and landscape, all are one;
They stand alone on the wooded hill.
Love is the reason why we come
And wisdom to direct love's will.

* *East Leicestershire*

BILSTONE GIBBET*

Forgotten once and for all
Without this wood -
A name, like the wind passing,
not understood.

This stock crannied with cuts,
Channelled and scored,
Its iron clamps still rattling
Where the wood was gored,

Stands by the wayside, survivor
Through time–
The oak bent to exhibit
The spoils of crime;

Its rings in place, its bolts
And rust-flecked hasps;
A ghost of a cage in the shape
Of the corpse it clasped!

I have seen the like in a cell
Deep underground,
And saw in my mind suspended
Flesh and bones bound,

And thought how the wind and the rain
Peel away rind;
The birds descend; across the fields
Call to their kind;

And wondered then with what right
The iron and oak
Be conscripted to act out of nature
This role in man's work.

Here it was barren, the post
And the place;
Barely a sign, pathetic,
Its meaning effaced;

And yet in the worrying wind
One held one's breath;
The roadside alone seemed poised
For inexorable death.

The briars and grass, the upland
Stretching away,
All seemed in their turn to fuse
The past with today.

And a name still rattled down wind,
Otherwise lost;
John Massey, for murder, your body
Was hung on this post.

*John Massey was convicted at Leicester Assizes in 1800 of the murder
of his wife and daughter. After his execution, his body was gibbeted at
Bilstone, west Leicestershire, near the scene of the crime.*

Primus Fecit X*

Tiler
in tanned hide, moulding mud,
made ten.

This first son of his father
says so himself; he lets it be known
to whoever should happen (we the unwitting)
to come across his comb-scratched script.

Now from the fabled past he is ours: deer-skin and smock,
sandals thonged, tied to a fine trade in a far land,
coining latin in a bleak swamp.

He works the flats, he of the clay-reared tribe
at the edge of the world; boxes the slime with bats
for thin brick, tiles and *tegulae;*
traps in the process beetles and stones and hair,
bakes to fire and back, takes
the blotches in his stride and the cracks;
cuts notches, scrapes with his toothed scalpel
for grip, throws it aside.

That's the lot.
Still, sufficient to ensure
that after a certain space we are known again
though ever so casually; but nothing's so strange
as isn't to the purpose.

I wonder, was it pride
in his work, or simply to make tally
with the overseer's record that he combed his cross?
A message to his mates? Proof for his boss?
Or was it after all something revealed
to our millenium?

Enough to know that Primus made it, he made it well,
and there were ten of them.

*Inscription on a Roman flue-tile found in Leicester.

THE GARDEN

The garden baffles me –
I am not used to its anyhow resilience;
Perhaps if I let it be
It would spring to my purpose with all its common sense.

The garden breeds –
Why, then, should I catalogue a wealth of plants?
Somewhere among the weeds
It keeps close the key to its true accounts.

Yes, there is phlox and fuchsia,
Cottage-garden stuff, and creepers on the wall,
An urn for a feature,
Grass, groundsel and twitch, and a greenness over all.

So what? you may ask,
The garden is nothing but nature in a frame;
Ah, but its real task
May be to counter-wild the cultivated strain.

Allow it to be then,
Profess to the store that it owes –
Leaves, roots and rhizomes and rings, seedlings and stems,
And that careless abandon of life where anything goes.

DONKEYWISE*

This art by the flourishing Hunt's
a trifle contrived (you could say)
oozing its *oohs* and *aahs* for Nicholas Nyes.
It doesn't fool me with its path
to the church beyond, *beyond*
(always beyond),
as if such a distance were ever discovered
to be there in view
at such an angle through such a door;
and then the bowler-hatted boy
(Tom, Dick or Harry)
with cheeks of lint and a bale of grass
safely ministering to the knowing beast.

It's all too wise.
Donkeys aren't like that at all; they're just
hair and hoof, and leathery skin,
blurred eyes, olfaction and bowels,
piss, shit and bite;
and the chickens lumps of rump
which dart and fight...

Funny, though, there are Toms still about
and donkeys in pictures we like.

* *On a picture by the sentimental Edwardian painter,*
Walter Hunt (1861-1941)

VIDEO

Viewing again those figures against smoke,
the wounded, languorous eyes across crowds of cables,
the rouged, the ochred masks of faces in the shadows
(intending still to reformulate the equivocal style),
I feel what a counter it is to the disaffected streets.

They are codes of love which produce these distortions,
the curious handling of gratuitous abstract shapes,
cheekbones caringly arched, the insouciance, the parade
of the seen, never itself but always pure projection.
I am also biased, a confederate to contrivance and colour.

When a helm-like figure looked out over the imagined sea,
when the camera's deception produced that adorable image –
the passive impasto of *face* as the absolute –
it would have been the same then for the fathers and the children,
this ambiguous eloquence of transformation
confronting the dream we always take for ourselves.

PROTEST

When the bomb falls I shall be living
in the strategic city.
I shall run out on hearing the first echo
of the slammed door
to greet the quiet light.

No longer then the quaint thought
and the strange heart;
no longer someone else's torn ghost, no longer
a ghost; no longer, when the door slams,
a fable, a failure.
For once in my life, beyond all its weakness and candour,
an insolent clarity.

When the bomb falls I want to be there
in the strategic city.

In Memory of George Fraser*

Driving back late one summer evening
across two countries, the rain in fitful mood
vying with brilliant light across the windscreen,
we stopped, unplanned, under trees at Bredwardine.
The hillside gave the cue, and all the stones
fallen out calmly from their station
like abandoned cards in the shadowed greyness
of a tall church, where a warm steam rose
from the earth. We found the place and looked.
'Poor man,' he said. 'No...'– smiling again,
head to one side, eyes lit – 'not poor at all! '
And that was it: an implicated pause
earned from our climb through awkward grass
amidst graves and sunshine and all those last
hours of a long day.

Who would have thought then that the year ahead
would resolve at last the littleness of life?
– In a car, in a town, in armchairs by the fire,
talking of friends, the years, relationships,
worrying lines in public bars and shops,
the table-talk of tumbled memories;
or breaking bread, trance-like, every act
a vow to re-confirm it all afresh.

You talked of Venice when the dark came down
in bundles of black cloud over stark light,
of all that stranger light you couldn't track
in the hazy morning sun of the lagoon.
Even the music, a fine transparency, eluded,
those chaconnes of Albinoni, those concerti,
like the water a paradox of light,
or like the equivocation of the walls
solid, rippling, patched in patterned dust,
rising or falling, ephemeral or real?

You talked of Titian and of Veronese –
the magical *Tempesta* with that comfortable
naked woman on the rock suckling her child,
and the soldier looking on but unconcerned
(the wide gap of the picture in between),
and what the town should be lit up by lightning
in the clear moment of the whole enigma,
drawing us through to the broken column of ourselves
and why we should be here at all, you'd say.

It's always the edge of the just discernible
that we'd like to drift to and look into.
Your glee was warmer and your heart more fierce
when the predictable was forced and over-ridden,
and all the ruins not only for themselves
splendid, but for some inkling too in this
admixture of coincidence and form
that something else will be there to adventure.

So walking once in the city in your suit,
light grey, ruffled, the corona of your hair,
the flickered disarray of a handkerchief –
a musing figure, a figure past all striving,
but one to wander in the afternoon
among businessmen and the perpetual flow
from bridge to tower, from subway to the square;
but standing apart, interpreter, observer,
translating still the endless possibilities
of light and shade and the distanced panorama
of a world where time's suspended or not itself
or what it was when once you knew it burning,
where now the edges merge and the gritty blurs;

walking there, in the shade of a tall college,
you could have glimpsed a figure on the road
too occupied to stop – the one who since
regretted the unapproach; or again, one too
brief knowing (who guessed a final meeting?),

where commentaries were courteously delivered
like flickers of incongruous inspiration
out of the dark of knowing, the frown of feeling.

That was the last. But the first was far before,
far otherwise (since you were worlds apart),
but a kind of transmigration of ideas,
or – dare I say? – sympathies: once, when I wrote
out of compulsion towards nothing, no-one,
a kind of writing 'without matter, nameless'–
the self-abuse of all that juvenilia–
but strangely, of the London you remembered,
its towers and temples, colonnade and park,
Debussy heard from Imhofs along Oxford Street,
a Chinese jar revolving in its stillness,
or of some Turner painting – 'say a late one'–
or next to *Loot* at the Jeanetta Cochrane
some posters peeling from a subway wall
advertising Cohen at the Tate...

In all, the inconceivable design
of pretension's transformation into truth,
of a touched heart turned to its best craft
to shape the legend of its purposes:
a life lived richly fronting all its terrors–
all those inconsistencies and alarms
purposed from some ridiculous beginning;
and then the possibility of a shadow
dodging the traffic in a crowded street
(the nervous hand that stirred the slightest tremor)
on neither side known; except later,
except in a poem, except perhaps in a poem.

The poet and critic, G.S. Fraser, died in 1980. The style of some poems in his collection Conditions, *and some internal references to his "Epistle to a Young Poet" are alluded to in my poem.*